Discover the several functions of the wind and how you can harness these to fulfil God's plans for you

commanding the wind

DR. OMOBOLA JEFFREYS

Dr. Omobola Jeffreys' Book
Published by Homotayor Creativity World

Foreword

The book, Commanding the Wind, is clear, concise, and filled with valuable and insightful prayers.

Dr. Omobola Jeffreys has created a result-focused book that draws you in, but also leads you to pray efficiently with sustained vigour. She highlights how to harness the power from the wind through biblical examples, thus delivering a scripturally balanced petition.

This book is a must have for anyone looking to break through and gain freedom from pushbacks, setbacks and near success syndrome. It is not for the faint hearted; so, get ready to command the wind that will usher in a new dawn for you.

Pastor Dumebi Jeffreys

Contents:

3	Table of Contents
4	Acknowledgement
6	Wind Definition
6	The Wind Brings Freshness And Removes Staleness
9	The Wind Enables Motion And Gives Fast Track Access
12	The Wind Fans The Flame Of Destruction.
15	The Action Of Wind Resets The Brain Of The Oppresso
19	The Wind Causes Wreckage.
22	The Wind Can Bring An End To Affliction.
24	The Wind Operates In A Stealth Mode.
27	The Wind Can Blow Good Away.
28	Wind From The East Brings Destruction.
29	The Wind Can Pollute.
32	The Wind Can Blow Away Things Of Value.
33	The Wind Can Bring A Rising.
34	The Wind Exposes To Wastage And Elements.
35	The Wind Raises An Army.
37	Wind Can Prolong Journeys And Make Passage Difficu
39	The Wind Can Bring Clarity.
42	Wind Brings Beauty
43	Wind Manipulates Navigation
46	Negative Wind Makes The Best Skills Useless.
50	Combined Wind Brought Provision.
55	The Wind Restores
58	Wind Causes Major Life Changes
61	Wind Brings Power.
62	Wind Changes Seasons

Acknowledgment

The Holy God, The Source of all knowledge. Many times, I marvel how He loves me so. I consider it a unique privilege to be given access to great depth of understanding of His word. I owe Him my obeisance!!!To my husband, Pastor Dumebi Jeffreys, for covering and co-labouring with me, I am grateful for your leadership.

The wind is the power that makes a storm; a storm becomes naked and without strength once the wind is taken away. The wind makes waves bigger. Makes it scarier and this weakens the heart of the observers.

WIND DEFINITION

Wind is air in motion. Though unseen, it is an active part of the dynamics of the earth.

THE WIND BRINGS FRESHNESS AND REMOVES STALENESS.

The lack of wind means that there will be no freshness. As an undergraduate living in a self-contained room with a tiny window, I slept off whilst cooking one day, and burnt my pot of beans. For the next few weeks, I sprayed perfumes, body spray etc. I could neither stop nor remove the smell of the burnt beans from my clothes. I was embarrassed each time I turned up for a lecture. The smell of burnt food was obvious, and it stayed on me several weeks more because of the poor ventilation in my room. The blowing of the wind is meant to bring freshness; therefore a few things will happen if you are a poorly ventilated human being.

- *One can become stale and people will not want to be in one's presence.*
- *One can become faint due to lack of vitality.*
- *One can become dull due to lack of interaction or care.*
- *Impatient people may lose interest due to them not being willing to discover your real value and you may miss opportunities.*
- *You may start doubting your own value if you have no reminder for yourself.*
- *Dust settles on you and you become undervalued and overwhelmed by the fragrance of abandonment.*

No matter which one of these you have experienced, you can command the wind from the presence of God to blow upon your life and turn things around in the name of Jesus.

PRAYER POINTS:

- *Father, disconnect me from the source of every spiritual stench which has contaminated my freshness.*
- *Father let the wind from your presence blow on my life. Let it strip me of every spiritual odour which has stayed with me, thus discouraging good from coming to me.*
- *Let your wind clean away every fragrance of abandonment which has reduced my value and worth before my assessors.*
- *Let your wind sweep through me, refreshing me and making me whole, to give strength to my fainting heart.*
- *Lord, cause your wind to blow my delightful fragrance far and near into the presence of those who will do me good.*

Do you remember how you recognise the aroma of a familiar dish from afar? Yes, every food seller needs the wind, otherwise, the aroma from the food will be perceived only by your household which means that you are not able to make profit.

- *Starting from now, the wind from the presence of God will spread my fragrance beyond my local reach and advertise me to lands beyond my current circle of influence.*
- *The wind from the presence of God will give me an affiliation towards good. I shall be drawn to making profit; because of God's fragrance*

blowing towards me, I shall attract favour and favourable preference.

- As the wind blows beautiful fragrance into my life, I enforce sustained interest in my endowed goodness and skills as the lord blows away every dust and staleness to reveal me to the world.

- Every man and woman, every kingdom and organisation, every authority scheduled to do me good, wherever you are in the world, I draw you to my beautiful fragrance. It shall lead you straight to me.

- I command whatever is meant to profit me and enrich me, no matter how far away they are from me, by the wind from the presence of the lord, to blow its fragrance in my direction, for my guidance, so I will not waste time, seeking endlessly.

THE WIND ENABLES MOTION AND GIVES FAST TRACK ACCESS.

EXODUS 14:21, 26-27 (ESV)

Then Moses stretched out his hand over the sea, and the lord drove the sea back by a strong east wind all night and made the sea dry land, and the waters were divided.

Recently a plane flying from the United States of America to the United Kingdom completed a 10hour flight in 6hours; a hurricane across the Atlantic gave the plane a boost. The pilot found himself helped by the wind as it pushed the plane from behind. The plane was not flying faster but the opposition of the wind was reduced by a stronger wind; the flight was accomplished effortlessly, and they arrived earlier paying no extra fare. You cover more grounds and arrive without delay when you have speed. Imagine someone flying in to see their child delivered or say goodbye to a loved one; they have the advantage of early arrival when they have speed. You get rewarded more for the same labour when the wind helps you. You will now command the wind to hasten your journey towards purpose.

PRAYER POINTS:

- *Father, cause your wind to enable my movement forward in every aspect of my life where there has been stagnation.*
- *I glide into ease upon the wings of the wind where many are still trying to grasp their life's delays and setbacks.*

- *Every aspect of my life meant to give me easy access but have been contaminated, flooded like a swamp, and overpowered by generations before me, I command the wind from the presence of God to dry them up now and make my journey easy as your wind dried up the sea.*

"Delay is expensive; you waste time, your resources and may never catch up with the timeline required for progress."

- *I command the wind from the presence of God to blow away every delay on my path towards destiny.*
- *My speed from now will align me with helpers who are scheduled to help me.*

There is one wind that will function in many capacities; the same wind that dried up the sea divided it into two, giving access to the children of God.

- *Lord, I order one strong wind which will sort out every outstanding steps separating me from my promise land.*

You simply cannot do it by yourself the things that take time. If it took a strong east wind all night to roll back the sea, how long will it take you to accomplish those? You need the wind.

- *Lord, everywhere the door of access was shut in my face even though I followed your instruction, and, being well within your plan, I now* stretch my hand over this sea of delay and command it to give way to me.

- Every resistance which has limited me going forward by the strong east wind, I drive you back in the name of Jesus.

It is good to know that there was an expressway at the bottom of the sea all this while.... they only needed it cleared and visible.

- Father, cause your wind to blow into view every route of escape that has been hidden but was meant to lead me out of my present predicament.

2 Samuel 22:16
The lord spoke strongly. The wind blew from His nose. Then the valleys of the sea appeared, and the foundations of the earth were seen.

- Lord, let the wind from your nostril expose every foundation of events which have remodelled my life outside your plan.
- Today, I ask that the wind from the presence of the lord will blow at every sea that has overwhelmed me and show me the way out of misery for every challenging situation that has kept me bound.

THE WIND FANS THE FLAME OF DESTRUCTION

Psalms 107:25 (NLT)
He spoke, and the winds rose, stirring up the waves. John 6:18 (NCV)
by now a strong wind was blowing, and the waves on the lake were
getting bigger.

The wind is the power that makes a storm; a storm becomes naked and without strength once the wind is taken away. The wind makes waves bigger. Makes it scarier and this weakens the heart of the observers.

A few years ago, a young child was bitten by an insect. The parents could not decide early whether they should do something about it. They let it be. After some days, the area where she got the sting started to swell, then it moved to the whole limb, then both legs. Before long, it affected the whole body. Her kidneys shut down and bone marrow failed. This was not meant to be so.

It was a small insect bite, but the wind gave power to the rain and it became a storm.

Many people are confronted with simple life challenges, but they grow bigger and beyond what they can manage right under their watch.

For instance, you have a condition which requires medical help, but you do not have money, whilst this is ongoing, the condition deteriorates to where you need even more intervention.

When power has been given to affliction, a small rain backed by wind becomes magnified into a storm that destroys.

PRAYER POINTS

- *I silence every storm which has been blowing in my life, hereby causing me to suffer losses.*
- *To every wind which has given power to the storms of my life, I speak peace, be still.*
- *Every simple (health problem, marital situation, financial, emotional, academic) situation which has become complicated due to external negative interference and manipulation.... Today, the light of God's countenance will shine upon me and you will be simplified for resolution.*
- *I take the pang away from every wind of affliction which has been enabled to cause me continuous pain.*
- *Every simple rain that is falling upon my land but has been hijacked by the wind and changed into storms, today, I quieten you down permanently.*
- *Every wind blowing at my life, making my heart fail, and making my God seem small, today, I take power away from you.*

A change in direction is meant to be easy, you just need a stronger power. But some turnarounds are easier than others. whatever results you are seeing depends on the wind blowing towards you.

THE ACTION OF WIND RESETS THE BRAIN OF THE OPPRESSORS

Exodus 10:12-17 (CEB)
Then the lord said to Moses "stretch out your hand over the land of Egypt so that the locusts will swarm over the land of Egypt and eat all of the land's grain and everything that the hail left." so Moses stretched out his shepherd's rod over the land of Egypt, and the lord made an east wind blow over the land all that day and all that night. When morning came, the east wind had carried in the locusts. Pharaoh called urgently for Moses and Aaron and said, "I've sinned against the lord your God and against you. Please forgive my sin this time. Pray to the lord your God just to take this deathly disaster away from me."

Moses was a human being like us, he received instruction and did accordingly. Following this, he commanded the wind with the use of his hand and right before his eyes, Pharaoh saw a demonstration of power that made him rethink his actions!!

PRAYER POINTS
- *Lord, cause your wind of correction to notify every oppressor of y destiny of your impending judgement.*
- *Lord, as I follow your instructions today, I command the wind from your presence to blow amongst the camp of the wicked who have declared war on me and my household.*
- *Lord, let your wind usher destruction of all that they have relied upon as their agent of destruction.*

The Israelites had been in bondage for several years......one hand-lifting by Moses, a wind blew for 24 hours - all day and all night and years of slavery was challenged.

- *No matter how long I have been held bound or this case has been going on, Lord, you do not need that same duration of time to turn things around. Tonight, the wind from your presence will turn things around for me suddenly.*
- *Lord, your wind will challenge all that has kept me bound from moving forward and walking into my inheritance.*

Jonah 4:8
During the day, the lord sent a scorching wind, and the sun beat down on Jonah's head, making him feel faint. Jonah was ready to die, and he shouted, "I wish I were dead!"

- *Lord, cause your scorching east wind to blow and the sun beat down on every hand that has stubbornly upheld my travail in delay there are some changes and repentance that do not happen until God has warned on several levels,*
- *Lord, I give you permission to correct my oppressors on all levels until they repent and change their ways.*
- *Lord, I have been threatened, my home, health, job, career, finance, and my ideas also; I have received threats of being chased, caught, plundered, and destroyed. By your breath tonight, let the weapons of heaven be activated to come to my aid.*

When the wind from God blows in His anger, things that

were meant to serve suddenly turn against one. The sea was meant to be a means of transportation, it became a grave.

- Lord, I command the wind from your breath to start waging war against every man or woman who has threatened all that you have allocated to me.
- The wind of God will blow everything in nature to start to work contrary to their peace and comfort.

Some have not threatened, they are operating quietly, Lord, you see them all....

- Lord, every army standing against and resisting my progress, I command the wind to blow the sea upon the shores where they lay in wait and sink them permanently.

When the wind fights for you, the amazing thing is that you do not go anywhere near the opponents...it is a silent operator, all you see are results.... what is attacking them cannot be seen..... We have had personal experience of the angels delivering the blows , when they cannot be seen by the ordinary eyes.

- Lord, blow your invisible wind and make it cause chaos and confusion within the camp of them who have promised to afflict me.

Isaiah 29:2-8

from deep in the earth, you will call out for help with only a faint whisper. then your cruel enemies will suddenly be swept away like dust in a windstorm. I the lord all-powerful, will come to your rescue with a thundering earthquake and a fiery whirlwind. every brutal nation that attacks Jerusalem and makes it suffer will disappear like a *dream when night is over. Those nations that attack Mount Zion will suffer from hunger and thirst. they will dream of food and drink but wake up weary and hungry and thirsty as ever people will have time to focus on you only when they are free, when they are tied down with their own issues, you become less of a priority.*

PRAYER POINTS

- *Today, I authorise heaven to allocate a windstorm to sweep away every cruel enemy sworn to my destruction.*
- *Lord, come to my rescue with thundering earthquakes, and fiery whirlwinds to deliver me.*
- *Every wicked and brutal nation that attacks me will disappear like in a dream.*

Our God is a show-off God....He sent different levels of scare ahead of his arrival; meanwhile, we have found a good use for His show-off.

1 Kings 19:11
And a great wind from the presence of the lord tears mountains and breaks rocks into pieces.

- Every good and benefit due me, hidden inside and under spiritual rocks and effigies, today, Lord, break the rocks and mountains and deliver them to me.
- Every rock which has stood in my path to restrict me, I command the wind from the presence of the Lord to break asunder every rock which has stood in my path.

THE WIND CAUSES WRECKAGE

Ezekiel 27:26-27 (GNT)
When your oarsmen brought you out to sea, an east wind wrecked you far from land. All your wealth of merchandise, all the sailors in your crew, your ship's carpenters and your merchants, every soldier on board the ship— all, all were lost at sea when your ship was wrecked.
For you to understand what happened in the scriptures above, you first need to grasp what was the state of the ship and its journey before it was wrecked by the wind.
Many people set out to go to great places in life and their journey goes smoothly until they meet one major set-back and they begin to struggle to get back on their feet; all within a ship is lost when it is wrecked by the wind ...Read the accounts of the ship below, its glory before it was attacked.

Ezekiel 27:33-36 (NCV)
When the goods you traded went out over the seas, you met the needs of many nations. With your great wealth and goods, you made kings of the earth rich. But now you are broken by the sea and have sunk to the bottom. Your goods and all the people on board have gone down with you. All those who live along the shore are shocked by what happened to you. Their kings are terribly afraid, and their faces show their fear. The traders among the nations hiss at you. You have come to a terrible end, and you are gone forever.'''

PRAYER POINTS

- *I forbid every wind targeted to wreck my ship, no matter your source and the purpose of the wreckage, you will have no access or cause me losses.*

- *There shall be no loss of my wealth or merchandise or that which I have laid up for my future prosperity and comfort.*

- *There shall be no loss to those who serve with me, whether in my home, marriage, career, within my household, in my business and the friends who are my companions on my life's journey.*

- *There shall be no loss to my builders, who make sure that I am on my feet and staying afloat. I forbid the wind of destruction from blowing at those who help me get back on my feet and make life comfortable for me.*

- *There shall be no loss to the people whose success are tied to mine. My children for whom God has given me the right of care, my husband whom God has sent me to help to achieve a great destiny. No negative wind shall blow at you; I possess the gates of your destinies and forbid harm from coming to you.*

I have been a medical doctor for over 20 years, I help people keep healthy, but not everyone can benefit from my expertise and years of knowledge. Even if one were to suffer any life problems, let there be help available, at least.

- *Wind shall not wreck me far away from where my help will reach me!!!! I shall not be separated from those who have the capacity to assist and those willing to help me.*

- *Wind of life, you shall not blow me far from my allocated and* designated help, and you will not blow them away from me.

- The lord has made me an answer to the needs of many in this world, no wind shall therefore turn me into a tragedy. I was designed to be a help to nations, thriving to the point of giving help to others, I shall not swap places with those I am allocated to help.
- I disallow you, every wind that turns a glorious life to a terrible end, you shall not find a foothold in my life. I shall now have time to recover and gain grounds as I move towards restoration.

THE WIND CAN BRING AN END TO AFFLICTION

Genesis 8:1-2 (GNB)

God had not forgotten Noah and all the animals with him in the boat; he caused a wind to blow, and the water started going down. The outlets of the water beneath the earth and the floodgates of the sky were closed. The rain stopped.

PRAYER POINTS

- *Lord, it does not matter how long I have been in this situation, I know that you have not forgotten me, please cause your wind to blow on me now.*

- *God, the waters of trouble have swept me up to my throat, make your wind blow, so that the waters which seek to subdue me will dry up.*

- *The wind of the lord will blow upon me today and dry up the springs underground that has sustained my pains and sorrows.*

- *By the breath of the lord, I command the clouds of destruction and stagnation in the sky to stop pouring its rain upon me and my household.*

The wind can manipulate human navigation, insects, and even non-living things. The east wind brought locusts; it brought destroyers and afflictions direct to them.

THE WIND OPERATES IN A STEALTH MODE

John 3:8 (MSG)
You know well enough how the wind blows this way and that. You hear it rustling through the trees, but you have no idea where it comes from or where it's headed next.

The wind is at work whether you see it or not, apart from its sheer strength, it's the fact that you can't even see it coming that makes the wind scary. It is what you see you can fight, isn't it?

The wind of the wicked is unpredictable, so also is the one we order. The enemy should not be able to determine our area of attack as we operate in stealth mode.

Confuse the enemy today in the place of prayers.

PRAYER POINTS

• *Every wind that has blown into my life, with or without me seeing or knowing, taking precious possessions away from me, today, in the same way you stole discreetly, I restore discreetly.*

The wind is not predictable, cannot be monitored; even the best scientific tool can get it wrong sometimes.

• *Lord, no man or woman, born of a woman will be able to monitor nor divert any wind you have scheduled to bring me ease and increase.*

The wind responds to the highest bidder; when you want to fan a flame and make it bigger, you send the wind. When you wish to blow out a candle, you send wind.

- *Wind, your roles are dependent on your sender's desires and rights; upon my right as an heir of the kingdom of God, today, I command a reversal of your role in every contrary wind sent out to cause me harm and distress and blow my life out prematurely.*

The wind decides the quality of your catch; it can also scatter what has been gathered. It decides which fish you catch and in what quantities.

There is always a cold wind after a storm, this cold wind causes pressures to rise in waters, making the fish go into hiding. The wind decides the tides!!!!! Tides affect deep sea fishing, dictating the concentration of fishes in one place, called "whirlpool". There is a wind that makes results difficult.

- *Lord, from today, I bring to a stop every wind which has triggered cascades of losses for me.*
- *Father, today, I command the wind to blow the waters in my favour, bringing to me rare and profitable catches.*

Have you ever seen those punished by the wind? They lose a precious piece of paper and as they reach out to pick it, the wind carries it farther?

Some people are chasing after the same things for years, just when it seems within their reach, the wind blows and carries it farther, they start again...

- *I still every wind that has made my results further out of my reach.*
- *Father, I address every wind which has caused me repeated labour by scattering my results, leaving me without a reward for my labour. Today, I take power away from you and I decree, peace be still.*

Wind makes it impossible to catch up...just as you thought you have touched it, it moves again.

- *Father, I am tired of repetitive failures; things and positions move just before I lay hold on them. From tOday, every wind that blows, moving the goalposts for my success, I command you to be permanently still.*
- *I will catch up and lay hold on that which I am due, my hand will reach and retain good, in the name of Jesus.*

THE WIND CAN BLOW GOOD AWAY

Job 1:19

Suddenly a great wind came from the desert, hitting all four corners of the house at once.

Wind blew and knocked out the walls of Job's human investments and his children. Some people need the wind to blow away the resources of those who oppress them; Haman's problem was that he was rich; he offered to pay to destroy the people of God.

Haman had money and a position of influence; he could pay for the destruction of the Jews. Esther 3:9. He told the king, not to worry, that he would finance it himself.

PRAYER POINTS

- *For every man or woman whose riches or positions have enabled them to victimize me, and keep me bound, lord, I activate the wind from the east to start to knock down the walls of whatever has empowered them to oppress me. Beneath their wings lord, take power away from their flight.*

- *I deplete their stores and I command that which enables them to be plundered.*

- *Every wind which has blown at me and all that is mine, taking away good from me, today, I command you to stand still and oppress no further.*

WIND FROM THE EAST BRINGS DESTRUCTION

The East wind comes from a burning hot desert and it brings drought. When the land is dry, nothing planted in it thrives. As moisture is necessary for vegetation to thrive, roots find it difficult to penetrate the ground. The vegetations there ceased to grow. Both land and seed must have enough moisture for you to have a great reward.

PRAYER POINTS

- Lord, my land has been afflicted with dryness, I bring to a total end to every wind that has brought drought into my life.

- I ban every further wind, which has been scheduled or sent to afflict my land thus making it difficult for my effort to flourish within the land.

- I resist every wind afflicting my seed-making them die before they see the light of day.

THE WIND CAN POLLUTE

Growing up, we lived slightly lower than our neighbours and I hated the rainy days; at times, the wind from the rain would blow their rubbish into our compound, leaving us to clean up the mess they had left unattended. Some lands are clean and innocent, until they are polluted by winds which have carried dirt from afar.

PRAYER POINTS

- *I forbid every wind that will turn my beautiful habitation to a place of regret.*

Abigail was okay, she was pleasant and beautiful until Nabal came; he almost infected her destiny with his foolishness.

- *Any man who has carried a contamination that will overwhelm me and cause me regrets will not find me attractive.*
- *From today, wind, you shall cease to pollute my land. I shall no longer mop up the mess from surrounding territories.*
- *I will not inherit transferred calamity and chaos.*

A traveller with eyes on the mark need not rejoice if they do not control the wind, because it can upgrade their struggle without any prior notice.

- *I forbid every wind that will contaminate my vision taking away my clarity and ability to reach my mark of glory.*

You face difficulties sometimes because people find it easy to lodge complaints that are taken as credible against you.

- *An unpleasant wind from the presence of the Lord will accompany every testimonial against my progress. They shall lose credibility and they shall not hold anyone's favour.*
- *Every accusation levied against me on the ground of wickedness will lack credibility.*
- *Every beautiful report regarding me will start to enjoy a fragrance of heaven, giving it a welcoming credibility.*

A house is dignified if it has a cover; no matter how well dressed you are, a wind when it blows, can disgrace you. Wigs blown away; dresses blown up!!!! It carries away your cover.

THE WIND CAN BLOW AWAY THINGS OF VALUE

A hot wind dries up streams and rivers.

Hosea 13:15,16

Even though Israel flourishes like weeds, I will send a hot east wind from the desert, and it will dry up their springs and wells. It will take away everything of value.

Streams feed a city!!!! If they dry it up, the city will starve to death. Wells are a reliable constant source.

PRAYER POINTS

- *I put an end to every hot wind which has been sent into my life to dry up my springs of fresh water.*
- *Every spring that is meant to nurture my land, but has been dried up by hot wind, today, I restore you to full capacity.*
- *From today, I disallow every wind that has a reputation of taking valuable things from my life.*
- *I shall no longer lose my family members due to premature death.*
- *I shall no longer lose money.*
- *I shall no longer lose credibility.*
- *I shall no longer lose my honour.*
- *I shall no longer lose my testimony.*
- *I shall no longer lose my health.*
- *I shall no longer lose my profitable relationships.*

THE WIND CAN BRING A RISING

A balloon is flat on the floor when empty but becomes visible once filled with air.

PRAYER POINTS

- Lord, upon the wings of the wind, I will soar into limelight where I will no longer be hidden and obscure.

Naturally, the heavy do not fly! The wind on its own is light but can carry heavy things.

Wind carries heavy things and gives them wings to fly; it makes them function beyond natural limitations. Some settle into this state. Whatever you see on the ground can fly, it only needs the right amount of wind.

- Naturally, no one in my generation has crossed this line of greatness **(PLEASE ADD YOUR NAME/ THE GENERATIONAL CHALLENGE HERE)**, upon the wings of the wind, I shall defy the boundaries that limited my counterparts and predecessors.
- From today, I am enabled to operate beyond my ancestors.
- Every physical limitation, today, Lord, I climb on the wings of the wind to go far above such physical limitations.
- I am aided by the wind; I move beyond borders and defy traditions.

THE WIND EXPOSES TO WASTAGE AND ELEMENTS

Job 30:15 (NLT)

I live in terror now. My honour has blown away in the wind, and my prosperity has vanished like a cloud.

A house is dignified if it has a cover; no matter how well dressed you are, a wind when it blows, can disgrace you. Wigs blown away; dresses blown up!!!! It carries away your cover.

PRAYER POINTS

- From today, I silence and reverse every wind that has exposed me to shame and dishonour.
- From today, the wind of shame will not blow at me or bring dishonour.
- I erect guards in place to resist every exposure by wind, that will bring me disgrace
- The Lord shall raise a standard against every storm targeted at me , powered by wicked wind
- I shall not be exposed to elements that waste
- I shall abide in the cover of God's safety , hidden from affliction through undue spiritual exposures.
- I shall not expose myself, my marriage , my family, my finance , my health to affliction by the wind of the wicked
- I maintain a girl grip on all that God has committed into my care, I shall not give occasion to the enemy to waste .

THE WIND RAISES AN ARMY

Ezekiel 37:7-14 (NCV)

So I prophesied as I was commanded. While I prophesied, there was a noise and a rattling. The bones came together, bone to bone. I looked and saw muscles come on the bones, and flesh grew, and skin covered the bones. But there was no breath in them. Then he said to me, "prophesy to the wind. Prophesy, human, and say to the wind, 'this is what the lord God says: wind, come from the four winds, and breathe on these people who were killed so they can come back to life.' ``So I prophesied as the lord commanded me. And the breath came into them, and they came to life and stood on their feet, a very large army. Then he said to me, "Human, these bones are like all the people of Israel. They say, 'our bones are dried up, and our hope has gone. We are destroyed.' so, prophesy and say to them, 'this is what the lord God says: my people, I will open your graves and cause you to come up out of your graves. Then I will bring you into the land of Israel. And I will put my spirit inside you, and you will come to life. Then I will put you in your own land. And you will know that I, the lord, have spoken and done it, says the Lord.'"

Why was there slaying? Because in the slain, there was an army? There was a lot happening in that scripture, but we can see that there was no completion until the wind was ordered.

PRAYER POINTS

- *Lord, I know that you have been at work in my life, even though the results have taken time to show, today, in obedience, I prophesy to the wind, come from the four winds of the earth, and breathe upon the work of the lord in my life and bring it to completion.*

  The bible reported that it happened immediately.

- *Lord, it has been a long wait, as I have spoken, right now, I receive an immediate answer which will shock even me.*

The bible reported that the wind brought the army back to life...most of us have armies that are sick or even dead, today. It is up to us to bring them back to life. All you need to do is command the wind to bring them back to life.

- *Every army that is due to stand in a place of my defence but has been sent to premature death, today I revive you with the breath of God.*
- *Every help and assistance I am due to benefit from, but has been tied down and made inaccessible, today, in Jesus name, by the breath of the almighty, I reinstate you back to life.*
- *I command re-connection of all that is needed for me to be helped again.*

The Lord says that after you are back to life, he will put you in your own land.

- *Father, as promised, as your breath restores me to life, please establish me in my own land where I can thrive without disturbance.*

WIND CAN PROLONG JOURNEYS AND MAKE PASSAGE DIFFICULT.

Acts 27:4-15

They set out for Italy, from day 2, strong headwinds made it difficult for the ship to stay on course, making them divert their journey. Several days of slow sailing, the wind remained against them still diverting journeys. They lost a lot of time, exposed to more risks.

The first counsel came warning of shipwreck, loss of cargo and danger to life; but they compared based on experience, instead of listening to the person with the up-to-date information. Light wind started but it changed abruptly, and the named wind blew them out to sea!!!!

The loss was eventually controlled, the worst fear of any sailor. From vs 18, cargo loss, ship's gear, no sun, no stars, no hope, no food; they were so worried that they could not eat. The final part in Vs 21, they should have listened; 2 weeks later, planks and debris from the broken ship were all that was left.

PRAYER POINTS

- *Lord, you know the diary of every destructive wind, forbid me from moving on the day they are set to destroy as I do not intend to suffer loss.*
- *Lord, I align myself with the navigation of heaven, my journey will not be delayed due to winds on their own errand.*

- *I decree that no contrary wind will expose me to a cascade of losses.*
- *My ears shall be open to hear and heed to warnings from heaven which will save me from the impact of contrary wind.*

Light wind quickly changed to strong wind; suddenly, what started as a light problem got upgraded.

- *Father, my life, family, my business, my body, my marriage shall not be a training ground for stormy winds.*
- *I decree that no wind of life will turn my place of glory to debris of survival.*

THE WIND CAN BRING CLARITY

Job 26:13
By his breath, the heavens are cleared (made cleaner, clutters removed) using the winds to move clouds.

Have you ever seen a dark cloud? It creates poor visibility everywhere; then a soft wind moves the cloud and boom - you know where to put your foot.

PRAYER POINTS

- *Lord, I command the wind from your breath to clear every dark cloud preventing me from seeing clearly, thereby making me prone to errors and mistakes.*
- *I command the wind from the presence of the lord, to disperse every gathering of dark clouds which have limited me being recognised for the greatness you have put in me.*

Dark clouds prevent the plants from benefiting from the full rewards of sunshine. The rays of the sun are meant to light and warm you up, but you get withered by the heat without the benefits of the rays; the people watching assume you are okay, but no, you are not. Such people work in the central bank, but salaries are not regular; they have the oil without the glow.

- *Lord, the breath of your nostrils will clear everything hindering me from enjoying the full benefit of my current placement; at work, at home, in my family, in my businesses; that which is dripping intermittently will start to soak me to wetness.*

Some clouds are not dark, but they are thick; those clouds you do not want to meet on a flight; they cause turbulence. You are never sure if you are safe or not.

- *I command the wind from the presence of the lord to clear every wind of turbulence making me troubled in places where I should have rest all around me in my marriage, in my marriage, home, job, with my friends and in my health. Today you are okay, tomorrow not symptoms.*

When heaven is cleared, the skies pour clean water to refresh, no contamination. Some suffer recurrent miscarriages; the source keeps yielding defective seeds. freshness pours from the skies when dark heavy clouds move.

- *Lord, by your wind, I refresh and sanctify my source. it shall no longer produce defective seeds; I shall no longer be fed from a contaminated source.*

Wind makes it impossible to catch up...just as you thought you have touched it, it moves again.

WIND BRINGS BEAUTY

Job 26:13 (CSB)

By his breath, the heavens gained beauty.

PRAYER POINTS

- *Lord, by your breath, I gain beauty; the clouds which have covered me are moved away swiftly.*
- *From today, I gain recognition many; shall begin to see in me the greatness that they did not appreciate before now.*
- *Even those who have despised and disregarded me will start to see me in a new light, and they will give me value worth my while.*

When the skies are dirty with contaminated clouds, the little shine you have acquired appears rusty; like dirty rain on a white car which worsens the defects.

- *Lord, let your breath restore my shine and promote me this season, as you clean every stain that is hindering my shine from being effective. Lord, I give you permission to restore me to my original state of glory after clearing the sky.*

WIND MANIPULATES NAVIGATION

Exodus 10:13-14
So, Moses raised his staff over Egypt, and the lord caused an east wind to blow over the land all that day and through the night. When morning arrived, the east wind had brought the locusts. for the locusts covered the whole country and darkened the land. they devoured every plant in the fields and all the fruit on the trees that had survived the hailstorm. not a single leaf was left on the trees and plants throughout the land of Egypt.

The wind can manipulate human navigation, insects, and even non-living things. The east wind brought locusts; it brought destroyers and afflictions direct to them.

A while later in verse 19 of the same scriptures, the west wind sent locust packing; it navigated the locust out of the afflicted land!

PRAYER POINTS:
- Whilst I slept, not paying attention to God's instruction, the enemy took advantage of my disobedience and plundered my land; tonight, I obtain mercy needed to reverse every damage done.
- I command the wind of God to stop every further navigation into my land, which has deprived me of joy and fulfilment, causing me distress and losses.
- The wind of God redirect out every destroyer ushered into my land and all that God has committed into my care.

- *Father, I reverse every complication which has been ushered into my land due to the invasion which was not ordered by God.*

Your husband was meant to do you good, getting married was meant to do me good, the bible says that two are better than 1 for they have a better reward. Wind enhances the soaring of birds, it aids their navigation to higher grounds.

- *Lord, I receive an enhancement for climbing beyond my natural allocated skills.*

A change in direction is meant to be easy, you just need a stronger power. But some turnarounds are easier than others. whatever results you are seeing depends on the wind blowing towards you. The scientists say an object continues to proceed in the same direction until acted upon by an external force equal or stronger than it.

Jonah 1:4
God hurled a great wind.

PRAYER POINTS
- *The wind from the presence of the lord I give you permission to forcefully change my navigation from every venture that is driving me fast towards destruction.*
- *Wind from God's presence hasten my steps towards them that will do me good.*

- *Wind from the presence of God, slows me down from progressing towards any destruction that wastes prematurely.*

Jonah 1:12
The wind brought about a sudden break in the alliance Jonah made with the sailors, they were taking him further away from God's purpose.

- *Wind from the presence of the Lord, I give you permission to disturb my journey from every appointment, acquaintance, and alliance I have arranged with pain and heartbreak and regrets.*

Jabez was heading downwards. But a prayer just like this turned the direction.

- *Lord, if my life continues in this direction where it is going now, things are not looking good.*
- *Wind of God, turn my pain to blessing.*
- *The Wind of God, turn every restriction with which I have been afflicted into widened territories (opportunities, influence) - God stretches me to my limits.*
- *Wind of God, my abandonment to God's perpetual presence.*
- *Wind of God secure my territories from attack to protection from all evil.*
- *I receive a total navigation reset from the wind from the presence of God. It shall direct me in the way towards profiting.*

NEGATIVE WIND MAKES THE BEST SKILLS USELESS

Many people suffer from wasted effort, a disease commonly treatable in the presence of God.

You will address two things during this session **Wasted efforts** and **Failure at the brink of success.**

For each of these problems stated above, there is a wind for that. However, no matter how successful you appear to be, when your priority differs from or is at loggerheads with God's priority, he removes his hands of protection and the wind blows your effort away...

Haggai 1:9-11 (GW)

"you expected a lot, but you received a little. when you bring something home, I blow it away. why?" declares the lord of armies. "it's because my house lies in ruins while each of you is busy working on your own house. it is because of you that the sky has withheld its dew and the earth has withheld its produce. I called for a drought on the land, the hills, and on the grain, the new wine, the olive oil, and whatever the ground produces, on humans and animals, and on all your hard work."

Lord, for every loss I have experienced due to my selfish priorities, I obtain mercy and forgiveness. I align myself with God's purpose and priorities.

If you are not born again, or not accepted by Jesus but living in disobedience, this is the time to embrace repentance without this, prayer is a waste of time.

PRAYER POINTS

- *I hush every wind that has resulted in my skies withholding its dew and the earth its produce.*
- *By the breath of the lord, I reverse every drought in my land, on my hills and on my grains and whatever my land produces and my hard work.*
- *I ask that the Lord will breathe His dew upon my land and restore me to my ordained glory.*
- *Every oil that was designed to make me operate smoothly, but is now stale or dry, hereby introducing friction into my life , making me rub off hard on people and people on me , today, I ask that the breath of heaven restore you to me .*
- *New wine stands for harvest! Every harvest which has been withheld due to disobedience , I ask that the mercy of God will release to me now.*
- *Grain stands for financial and material blessings. Today , the wind from the presence of God will blow away the veil which has covered every blessing destined for me , but has been covered due to my ignorance and disobedience to God.*

Psalms 107:24-30

they saw what the lord had made; they saw his wondrous works in the

depths of the sea. God spoke and stirred up a storm that brought the waves up high. the waves went as high as the sky; they crashed down to the depths. the sailors' courage melted at this terrible situation. they staggered and stumbled around like they were drunk. none of their skill was of any help. so, they cried out to the lord in their distress, and God brought them out safe from their desperate circumstances. God quieted the storm to a whisper; the sea's waves were hushed. so, they rejoiced because the waves had calmed down; then God led them to the harbour they were hoping for.

Psalms 107:24-30 (CEV)
The ships were lifted into heights and plunged into depths, they lost courage and skills became useless. Skills looking incompetent because the wind lifted the waves of the sea.

PRAYER POINTS

- Every wind blowing difficulty my way, causing me to lose courage, bringing terror to me, tonight I silence you.
- I silence every troublesome wind, making useless my skills and expertise, making it look like I don't know what to do.

The wind made mockery of these strong men and they stumbled and staggered like drunken men.

- *Every wind targeted to make me become a laughingstock. I*

command you to cease from blowing.
- Just as the lord of hosts did, I calm every storm to a whisper and still every wave of affliction upon my life.

Acts 27:13-15 (GW)

when a gentle breeze began to blow from the south, the men thought their plan would work. They raised the anchor and sailed close to the shore of crete. Soon a powerful wind (called a northeaster) blew from the island. the wind carried the ship away, and we couldn't sail against the wind. we couldn't do anything, so we were carried along by the wind.

They started off as good, but later, small issues started coming up, then serious problems, then chaos

PRAYER POINTS
- Lord, I disturb and halt every cascade of chaos heading my way.
- I halt every process which has started with the purpose of making me lose track of all that you have committed to my care.
- Every ship which was allocated to take me to my joyful destination, but has been hijacked by the storms of life, I decree, find rest and harbour today in the name of Jesus.
- Lord, every violent wind which has taken over my life and left me without control, today, by the breath of the lord, I bring you to a calm.

COMBINED WIND BROUGHT PROVISION

Psalms 78:26-29 CEB
God set the east wind moving across the skies and drove the south wind by his strength. He rained meat on them as if it were dust in the air; he rained as many birds as the sand on the seashore! God brought the birds down in the centre of their camp, all around their dwellings. So, they ate and were completely satisfied; God gave them exactly what they had craved.

The winds combined forces; the east and the south wind gave satellite navigation to the birds. If he did it before, He can do it again.

Please note - God rained meat as dust or sand, He had it then, He has it now; why are you hungry?

Birds dropped right in the middle of the camp, not outside, they did not need to go hunt; they had ready meals and they ate and were completely satisfied.

PRAYER POINTS

- *Father, from now on, Winds from all over the earth will collaborate to provide for my household a rain of meat as dust in the air.*
- *Lord, the wind will usher and arrange the delivery for us to receive supply right at the place of need - you know my home address Lord, you know the address of my business; winds, deliver at my exact place*

of occupation.

- Father, following supernatural provision, our joy shall be full; the wind shall deliver my needs to my complete satisfaction.
- Lord, I command your wind to deliver everything that I crave in accordance with your plan for me.
- Lord, in obedience, I ask that the heavens to open upon all that is mine; he blessings of God makes rich and adds no sorrow, I surrender my will to yours and connect with the provision from above.

Whatever they needed was what dropped; not shoes, not bags but meat and food!

- Lord, you know my exact needs; I pull them off from the resources of heaven and I request that the winds of God will drop my exact needs to me.

Birds dropped right in the middle of the camp; not outside, they didn't need to go hunt. Ready meals were delivered to them. Some people will have help, but the location will discourage them from accessing it.

- I will not chase neither will I search far, I receive heaven's provision where it will be convenient for me to access it.
- Lord, the wind will usher and arrange the delivery for us to receive supply right at the place of need; you know my home address lord,

you know the address of my business, winds, deliver at my exact place of occupation.

The winds connived in purpose to meet needs.
- *Father, from now on, winds, authorities, individuals, countries, nations, people will collaborate to provide for my household a rain of meat as dust in the air. Organisations and authorities will rub minds and reach solid conclusions to help me.*

They ate and were completely satisfied.
- *Father, following supernatural provision, my joy shall be full, the wind shall deliver my needs to my complete satisfaction.*
- *Every provision I have given myself outside God's plans, tonight, I give you permission to waste them.*
- *Every provision that I have given myself which will stink and cause regrets in my future, lord, I relinquish them to you now for destruction.*

Proverbs 25:23.
As surely as a north wind brings rain, so a gossiping tongue causes anger!

The north wind brings forth rain which activates seeds that have been lying dormant.

PRAYER POINTS

I send the north wind upon my sweats; everywhere I have laboured, and my rewards have been withheld or denied, let the north wind start to usher rain to water it and bring it to the surface for reward.

The bible says that a workman is worthy of his wages.

- *Everything I have laboured upon but have been overlooked, the north wind will bring you back to life for recognition.*

When relocating into new lands; many who have been there for years before you may have stories of woe.

- *You will say, the ground may be hard, but I brought my own rain.*
- *The ground becomes soft when it rains, roots take to the ground easily; new plants which have not been well established get established with ease.*
- *Lord, I invite the north wind to soften my landing and give me ease of establishment.*

The bringer of comfort gets elevated when a land has been dried for a while.

- *As I usher in the north wind to bring rain unto my new territories, my arrival will herald comfort for as many as will acknowledge me and my God, announcing me as a solution bringer.*

When the wind fights for you, the amazing thing is that you do not go anywhere near the opponents...it is a silent operator, all you see are results.

THE WIND RESTORES

The wind has ears; they need a second shout sometimes.

Ezekiel 37:4-10 (GW)
Then he said to me, "prophesy to these bones. tell them, 'dry bones, listen to the lord 's word. This is what the almighty lord says to these bones: I will cause breath to enter you, and you will live. I will put ligaments on you, place muscles on you, and cover you with skin. I will put breath in you, and you will live. then you will know that I am the lord.'" so, I prophesied as I was commanded. while I was prophesying, suddenly there was a rattling noise, and the bones came together, one bone attaching itself to another. as I looked, I saw that ligaments were on them, muscles were on them, and skin covered them. yet, there was no breath in them. Then the lord said to me, "prophesy to the breath! prophesy, son of man. tell the breath, 'this is what the almighty lord says: come from the four winds, breath, and breathe on these people who were killed so that they will live.'" so I prophesied as he commanded me, and the breath entered them. then they came to life and stood on their feet. there were enough of them to form an exceptionally large army.

There was a lot happening, he prophesied the first time, but no completion until the wind was ordered. That's why you may need to do it again until you receive the right result.

PRAYER POINTS

- *Lord, I know that you have been at work in my life, even though the results have taken time to show, tonight, in obedience, I prophesy to the wind, come from the four corners of the earth, and breathe upon the work of the lord in my life.*
- *Every half-finished project which has made me look like a failure, today, I gain the breath of God to stir me towards completion.*

The wind brought things to life.

- *The wind from God's presence, bring my life to life, wind blow, that I may live!*
- *Every deadness in my finance, career, health, ministry, marriage come alive by the wind from God's presence.*

The bible reported that the wind brought the army back to life; many of us have armies, sick and dead, today, we will bring them back to life. We will command the wind to bring them back to life.

- *Every army that is due to stand in a place of my defence but has been sent to premature death, today I revive you with the breath of God.*
- *Lord, open the graves and let loose all my possessions which have been buried away from my reach.*
- *Help and assistance that I am due to benefit from, but has been tied down and made inaccessible, today, in Jesus name, by the*

breath of the almighty, I reinstate you back to life.

- I command re-connection of all that is needed for me to be helped again.

After coming alive, they stood up; to stand is to gain independence, to stand is to be recognized, to stand is to announce arrival.

- I welcome the wind of God to announce me in places where my rightful presence has been ignored.
- I gain total independence from all who have held me hostage due to my dependence on them.

The bible reported that it happened immediately.

- Lord, it has been a long wait, as I have spoken today, I receive an immediate answer which will shock me.
- The lord says that after you are back to life, he will put you in your own land.
- Father, as promised, as your breath restores me to life, please establish me in my own land.

Man did not become a living soul until the breath of God entered him.

- That singular last step required to seal my breakthrough, father, hasten it by your breath today.

WIND CAUSES MAJOR LIFE CHANGES

Wind decides results.

There is good wind, and bad wind, and they are controlled daily by powers which you may not be aware of, even though they exist. When good life but suddenly turns nasty; a wind has blown when life that has been a chore, suddenly things change for better, today a wind has blown night, we will be controlling winds movement.

Revelation 7:1-3 (CEB)
After this I saw four angels standing at the four corners of the earth. they held back the earth's four winds so that no wind would blow against the earth, the sea, or any tree. I saw another angel coming up from the east, holding the seal of the living God. he cried out with a loud voice to the four angels who had been given the power to damage the earth and sea. he said, "don't damage the earth, the sea, or the trees until we have put a seal on the foreheads of those who serve our God."

Those sent to damage were going to do so by their use of the wind. They were holding the four corners of the earth ,so no wind would blow. When the wind stops blowing what happens? - no freshness ,contamination persists , germs multiply illnesses and sickness have a fill day, stench accumulates, people are stressed, immunity goes down, body cannot fight off challenges, people succumb and get wasted.

One small action has ripple effects.

PRAYER POINTS

- *Whoever has been given legal right and power to damage me , my husband, children, home, ministry, career in the name of Jesus, I terminate your appointment of destruction in the name of Jesus.*
- *You will find it impossible to do me harm. Zipporah contended with the verdict regarding her husband!! I stand and declare the same for my husband, same for my children. You will not shorten my days and you will not contaminate my joy.*
- *Every wind that was meant to do me good, which has been held back, I release you now in the name of Jesus.*
- *Every cascade of wastage which has been set up to waste me by withholding the wind of God that brings me freshness, today, I halt you.*
- *Every stench which has been accumulated due to my wind being withheld, tonight, I flush you out by the wind from the presence of God, replacing you with a beautiful fragrance of his favour.*

Isaiah 40:29, 31 (GW)

He gives strength to those who grow tired and increases the strength of those who are weak. Yet, the strength of those who wait with hope in the Lord will be renewed. They will soar on wings. like eagles. They will run and won't become weary. They will walk and won't grow tired.

The wind decides the quality of your catch; it can also scatter what has been gathered. it decides which fish you catch and in what quantities.

WIND BRINGS POWER

The weakest of eagles just need to get into the air, and they glide; the winds take the stress of the flight away from them.

PRAYER POINTS

- *Lord, my wings are tired, and I am weak, in every place where I am meant to fly, power my wings by your wind from your presence.*
- *Lord, with the little strength remaining, I am taking a leap into the year; my small efforts will be accentuated by heaven's breath to lift me to heights beyond my capabilities.*

Some people are walking, but progress is not visible due to contrary wind.

- *In places where I am meant to walk, I receive strength and speed to walk against every contrary wind.*

WIND CHANGES SEASONS

Psalms 147:18 (MSG)
He launches His promises earthward how swift and sure they come! He spreads snow like a white fleece, he scatters frost like ashes, He broadcasts hail like birdseed—who can survive his winter? God can change seasons with his breath.

PRAYER POINTS

- Lord, you can change my seasons. My winter has been cold and harsh.

Breathe upon me this day lord, and

- Make my heart warm with love.
- Make the sun hit my face again and bring me radiance
- Make my flowers bloom again.
- Make the smell of freshness fill my abode again.
- Give your command and let the sun rise upon my grey skies one more time.

Genesis 8:1-3 (MSG)
Then God turned His attention to Noah and all the wild animals and farm animals with him on the ship. God caused the wind to blow and the floodwaters began to go down. the underground springs were shut off, the windows of heaven closed, and the rain quit. inch by inch the water lowered. After 150 days the worst was over.

PRAYER POINTS

- *The storm has been for long; Lord, turn your attention towards me and by your breath, dry up the flood of trouble around me.*

- *Whatever has sustained my troubles and trials, as the Lord breathes upon my, I command your source to dry up too.*

There is no doubt that you are now fully informed about the potentials you have. Being a child of God means that you can do all that He has demonstrated in the scriptures, using exactly His tools.

By now, you have moved ancient landmarks. You have been empowered to command the wind and get results you desire from life. We were not designed to be victims.

Henceforth, move forward, be bold. Take the gates of the enemies down and thrive without restraint. That was how God intended for it to be.

Keep commanding the wind.

Printed in Great Britain
by Amazon

21695606R00037